I FOUND A BABY RACCOON, WHAT DO I DO?

D1563307

DALE CARLSON
ILLUSTRATED BY HOPE M. DOUGLAS

WIND OVER WINGS PRESS
BICK PUBLISHING HOUSE

Text © copyright 1994 by Dale Carlson
© illustrations 1994 by Hope M. Douglas
Second Edition, 1995

Edited by Ann Maurer
Book design by Jane Miller
Cover design by Stan Park

With thanks to our veterinarian, Richard A. Alter D.V.M.

WIND OVER WINGS PRESS is a trademark of
BICK PUBLISHING HOUSE

ISBN: 1-884158-05-6 -- Volume 6
ISBN: 1-884158-04-8 -- 6 Volume Set

Printed by Royal Printing Service, Guilford, Connecticut, USA

Note

Even though helping hurt and distressed animals seems like an easy thing to do, it isn't always as simple as it looks.

It may require a legal permit in your state to raise and release wildlife.

Call your Department of Environmental Protection for advice, for the telephone number of your nearest local rehabilitator, for information on how you can get training and your own permit.

Contents

Acknowledgements

Our gratitude to the network of Wind Over Wings rehabilitators and its associated rehabilitator friends: Irene Ruth, founder and director of Suburban Wildlife; Cathy Zamecnik; Dawn and Job Day, Susanne Colten-Carey; Hope Douglas, founder and director of Wind Over Wings, and Tamara Miglio its president and our copy editor.

Our special thanks to Dan Mackey, publisher of Wildlife Rehabilitation Today Magazine, and to International Wildlife Rehabilitation Council for their inspiration and high standards of excellence.

And our thanks to Herb Swartz for his kindness and his computers.

I FOUND A BABY RACCOON, WHAT DO I DO?

WHY SAVE A RACCOON AT ALL?

Raccoons are common. So are human beings. Being endangered as a species is only one reason to save a life. Need is a more important reason. Being orphaned, injured, and helpless are reasons rehabilitators save lives.

Rehabilitators are dedicated to saving lives, not to deciding what forms of lives are worth saving.

Rehabilitators do not take prisoners and call them pets. Rehabilitators nurture, teach survival, feed, raise orphaned and injured wildlife, and return them in freedom to their natural habitats where and when this is reasonable.

Some people think raccoons are a nuisance. They hang around vegetable gardens, back yards, and restaurants, where there's food. Just like us. They eat everything they can get their paws on. Just like us. They're curious. Like us. They play, mate, and love their babies. Like us. Since they're so much like us, it may be time we enjoyed their company instead of persecuting them, trapping them, shooting them, and wearing their fur.

Backyard rehabilitators, many of whom are young people, understand wildlife is not ours to capture, experiment on, and destroy. They are people, surrogate parents, who do not take, but give back life.

REHABILITATORS UNDERSTAND THE LIMITS OF REHA-
BILITATION: ANY SICK OR INJURED ADULT, OR INFANT,
OR JUVENILE, NEEDS TO BE TAKEN TO A VETERINARI-
AN UNLESS YOU HAVE THE NECESSARY SKILLS.

WHY RACCOONS GET HURT

Raccoons get hurt from our attitudes about raccoons. Because we perceive them as a nuisance, we kill them. When they come in out of the cold to nest in our chimneys or garages, we trap, shoot, or poison them. When we suspect, even without cause, that they carry disease, we fear and persecute them out of ignorance and without information.

Raccoons are friendly and curious: many of us are suspicious and closed-minded.

Raccoons are willing to share habitat: we simply move in, take over, and evict.

Raccoons defend their nests and their young: we attack, not only with weapons, but with our dogs and cars.

Nature kills enough creatures: she doesn't need our help to decimate wildlife.

Learn to cap chimneys. Learn to deal effectively and intelligently with whatever problems wildlife may present. Learn to live with our wildlife and share the land with them. It can be done.

The answer is not always killing.

WAIT   WATCH   WARM

If you come upon baby raccoons on the side of the road, in a hollow log, under a porch, or anywhere else without their mother, watch for a couple of hours before you touch them.

To rehabilitate well, it is important to understand wildlife in the wild. In the case of raccoons, the mother may be nearby, or away feeding herself. Contrary to what people think, although raccoons are nocturnal, raccoon mothers are often out during daylight hours looking for food. This is normal, not a sign of anything wrong.

Raccoon babies often wake and leave the nest to search for their mother if she is gone too long. If you find babies by the road, put on heavy gloves, scruff them, and move them back away from the traffic.

Wait and watch. If no mother returns, collect the baby or babies — using heavy gloves, or if you do not wish to touch them, a small shovel — into a covered box.

Call your Department of Environmental Protection for the telephone number of a wildlife rehabilitator in your area.

In the meantime, warm your babies. You can keep them in the cardboard box. You can transfer them into a pet carrier, or stainless steel caging unit like a dog cage. Place a heating pad set on low beneath one third of the box. Line the container with paper toweling, but never colored newspaper (poison), and never cloth that shreds (to catch nails or choke in). Put a nonravelling towel, T-shirt, flannel cloth, or ski hat inside carrier to make the nest cosier for your frightened raccoon orphans to crawl into or under.

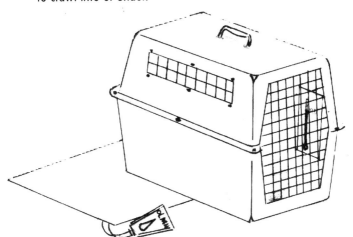

Later, at four to eight weeks, you will need a larger space, a cage unit 3'W x 3'L x 3'H for three or four kits in which is placed a smaller nest box of wood or cardboard for them to hide and feel secure. And raccoons love to play and climb. Hammocks, ramps, leaves, small branches create fun and a natural environment. (Remember: because of roundworm, do not use cage, nestboxes, toys, or anything else you have used in the care of raccoons for the care of any other creatures.)

If there is only one baby, place a ticking clock inside a piece of cloth to simulate the mother's heart. Don't be frightened. Baby raccoons won't bite you.

DO keep your baby raccoons warm. DO NOT feed them food or water right away.

Place your box of baby raccoons in a warm, dark, quiet place. Don't handle for a while. Let them rest. It is particularly important to keep the family dog away from the baby raccoons. For proper release, dogs must remain natural enemies.

Call: you will need the help of a licensed rehabilitator to care for the babies. This is true even if you are a practiced rehabilitator of other species but without experience with raccoons. This is true even more if a raccoon is injured or has symptoms of dehydration or illness.

In the case of a single baby, try to locate a companion. Unlike rabbit and squirrel mothers, raccoon mothers will often spend a year or more with their babies nurturing and teaching them. They are affectionate and sociable animals, and they need one another for company, to learn from, and for nurture, both in rehabilitation and afterwards in the nocturnal hours of their release. A companion will also lessen the temptation of the rehabilitator to become attached to the baby raccoon. It is better to encourage these intelligent, sociable, and affectionate animals to become attached to and to depend on each other.

YOUR RACCOON MAY BE HURT

Look at your raccoon to see if it seems hurt. Look to see if the limbs are placed properly in relationship to the body, not bent or twisted or hanging limply. Look to see if a limb drags or is crooked. Look to see if it can't stand properly or if one or more of its legs seem paralyzed. Look to see if there is any bleeding from an external wound. Look to see if blood flows from nose or mouth to indicate internal bleeding. Watch to see if your raccoon just lies there or breathing is rough. Watch for running bowel movements. (Healthy raccoon baby feces on a milk-based diet are formed and yellow in color; weaned, the stool is formed and brown.) Watch for discharge from nose or eyes.

Check for and remove with fingers any external parasites, like fleas, mites, or ticks.

You will need veterinary care to treat any injury or disease. Raccoons can be successfully treated for feline distemper, vaccinated against canine distemper, wormed for the roundworm *Baylisascaris procyonis*. Raccoons with signs of central nervous system disorders may have either canine distemper or rabies — or they may have been hit by a car and they may have no disease at all..

Call a trained rehabilitator if you know one, or call your Department of Environmental Protection, or your vet or local police who will have numbers of a wildlife rehabilitator near you, for help or advice before handling raccoons with neurological signs (convulsions, paralysis, facial twitching).

YOUR RACCOON IS HUNGRY

DO NOT feed your baby yet. A baby raccoon will react to a change from its mother's milk to your formula. Also, it may be dehydrated. Pinch to tent the skin. If skin is slow to return to normal position (greater than 1-2 seconds), your baby needs more than initial rehydration. Severe dehydration requires a vet's subcutaneous injection.

DO give even a healthy baby a special drink first called a rehydrating solution. Mix:

1 teaspoon salt		1/3 teaspoon salt
3 Tablespoons sugar	or	1 Tablespoon sugar
1 quart warm water		1 cup warm water

The above is a homemade solution. Commercially available electrolyte solutions such as Pedialyte can also be given.

You can offer the drink from a pet nurser or a nipple attached to a syringe for newborns. Use a human bottle for bigger kits. Raccoons have a strong sucking habit. Use premie nipples with small openings to prevent aspiration of the formula into the lungs. Offer 4cc's to 8cc's every fifteen minutes for the first hour. Check with your wildlife rehabilitator to find out whether to continue with rehydrating fluid only for the first twenty-four to thirty-six hours.

Make certain to keep your baby warm. Make certain to keep it resting quietly in a semi-dark place in between feedings to reduce stress. At this point, do not play with your rehabilitant.

QUIET is the watchword for captive babies.

NOW LEARN ABOUT RACCOONS IN THE WILD

While your baby raccoon rests, read about its needs, its ways of life in the wild, where it nests, what its food, play, and rest requirements are. A really good wildlife mammal book can be found at your public library if you don't own one.

AGES AND STAGES

You need to find out your raccoon's age to feed it the proper diet and house it in the proper way.

Here is a page of raccoons at different ages and stages of development.

Infant: Eyes and ear canals closed at birth, thin layer of fur, facial mask develops at 2 weeks, the tail color rings at 3 weeks.Eyes and ears open after 18 to 24 days.

Juvenile: At 6 weeks, guard hairs appear; crawling and walking begin at 4 to 6 weeks; at 7 weeks, climbing and exploring outside of nest; starting to follow mother and to forage at 8-12 weeks; in the wild, weaning begins before 16 weeks; by late fall may weigh 15 pounds.

Adult: Bushy-tailed; self-feeding; in the wild, weaned by 16 weeks; by late fall may weigh 15 pounds; may winter with mother and siblings; dormant, though not a true hibernation, in winter; yearling female may breed January to March; nocturnal, though may forage in daylight hours.

Different aged raccoons eat differently. Feed your raccoon properly to help it grow properly.

Your baby raccoon check list.

1. You have got your raccoon warm, rested, and calm.

2. You have seen it is not too hurt or stressed.

3. You have given it rehydration fluid.

4. You have identified your raccoon's age in your book and probably read as well about its natural habitat, natural foods, natural habits. All of this will help you care for it better.

FEEDING YOUR BABY RACCOON

You begin by mixing formula, just as you would for any baby mammal. The baby raccoon's formula is closest to a kitten's. KMR is recommended. Before the eyes are open, leave out the cereal and applesauce.

This is the formula we are using currently.
Mix:

2 parts water
1 part KMR (or use other kitten replacement formula powder and mix according to manufacturer's directions)
1 part baby rice or oatmeal or high-protein cereal
1 part applesauce (pure, no preservatives)
Theralin (vitamin and mineral supplement) (amount according to package directions, powder or liquid)

Aspirating formula can cause pnuemonia.
Raccoons suck strongly. Make certain your formula is not
too thin by adding cereal or use a nipple with a smaller
hole, or a syringe. Wash nipples and syringes thoroughly
between feedings, bottles every day. Make enough formula only for a twenty-four hour period. Hold baby upright
or on its stomach to feed: never on its back.

Feeding chart

Birth to one week 4-6 cc's every 2 hours (1 x at night)
1-2 weeks   6-8 cc's every 2 hours (1 x at night)
2-3 weeks   15-50 cc's every 3 hours
3-4 weeks   50-60 cc's every 3-4 hours
4-8 weeks   60cc's every 4 hours

IMPORTANT: Until eyes open, you must stimulate elimination and urination as raccoon mothers do. Gently rub the genital region with moistened cotton ball or tissue. Discontinue stimulation after two minutes whether elimination has occurred or not. You must do this until it becomes obvious babies are eliminating and urinating on their own. For bloat, submerge the lower body in warm water, and massage the tummy for about five minutes. Never overfeed: tummy should be round and firm as a marshmallow, not tight.

Weaning: At 5-6 weeks, begin to leave natural foods in cage such as moistened puppy kibble, high protein dog food, raw, boned fish, fruits, vegetables, insects, shellfish. By nine weeks, there should be no more bottle feeding. After weaning, offer dry kibble at all times, plus natural foods: grapes, berries, bananas, apples, walnuts, acorns, peanuts, eggs, crayfish, mealworm larvae, anchovies—all are much loved by raccoons.
Offer a bowl of water at all times. This is not only for drinking, but because raccoons prefer to wash their food before eating it. This has little to do with cleanliness. The water may sensitize their paws to whatever they are eating.

Remember: by 12 to 16 weeks, your raccoon should be ready for release.

PROPER HOUSING

You have already housed your raccoons in a small indoor cage with nest box. At eight weeks, around the time they are weaned, it is time for them to go into an outside caging unit. This should have a flight shelf for the nest box to encourage climbing, a sheltered area for bad weather and for the feeling of security. Give your raccoons a stimulating environment. Hammocks, hollow logs, tree trunks with branches for climbing, and a child's swimming pool for water play. Outdoor habitats can be made of 2x3's and wrapped with hardware cloth or chain link, including the flooring so that raccoons can't dig their way out and self-release. A double-door is advisable for the same reason. The size is typically 6'x8'x8' for three or four raccoons. Do not use pressure-treated lumber, it can be toxic.

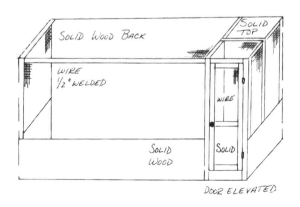

IMPORTANT: Because of raccoon roundworm which can be lethal to other species, including humans, the floors of raccoon habitats need to be of materials strong enough to allow for thorough cleaning with a blow torch or very strong disinfectants. Dispose of, preferably burn, all raccoon waste.

Again, a word about your domestic animals: Keep them away from your raccoons, not for their sake, but for the sake of your wild creatures. You are not only nurturer, but teacher. You don't want your raccoons approaching other people's pets after release and getting shot. Also, REMEMBER TO VACCINATE YOUR PETS AGAINST RABIES. It's the best protection you and your family has against your pet's bringing home the disease from infected raccoons in the wild.

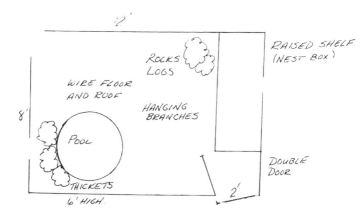

RELEASE

Before you release your raccoons, be sure you have been feeding them at dusk or later. They must be learning to eat at night.

Release your raccoons at about 16 weeks old. You can release a little earlier in a protected area if you want to provide backup food. Otherwise, they must be really self-sufficient, and no longer friendly even to you. Release sites should have water (stream, lake, marsh), woods with logs and trees for climbing and nesting, and they should be as far from human habitats, roads, cars, hunting sites as possible.

Check your weather forecast for three days of good weather. Leave a supply of dry dog food at the base of a tree at least for the first feeding.

Leave a large pet carrier with tempting food, nesting materials from the nest box, inside the larger habitat. If the raccoons do not enter willingly at dawn to nest so that you can close the carrier door, you may have to net them and place them in your carrier.

Release them late in August so they have plenty of time to establish a territory and nest, and put on a fat layer before winter.

Release them at dusk. Remember, they are nocturnal.

Release them in groups of two or more for company.

Go home happy. You have done well, given them a wonderful start.

Remember, the release is the most important after the saving part of rehabilitation. Wildlife is not ours to keep, but to help in its distress and let go.

You have done this.

Your raccoons may grow strong and release well.

Or one or more may not thrive, may hurt too much, and die. It is not your fault. Nature always knows more than we do. You did your best to protect its living and dying, kept it fed, warmed, and safe from predators. It is all you can do.

Except, now that you know how to help raccoons, help another one.

HOT TIPS FOR YOU

1. Don't handle a raccoon if you don't want to.

2. Call for help and advice.

3. Don't kidnap a baby raccoon. Watch for mother before rescuing.

4. Your goal in rescuing a raccoon is its release when possible. No critter wants a life prison sentence unless it is too hurt to survive.

5. If you find an injured adult raccoon, wear gloves.

6. Keep any critter away from your face.

7. Wash hands first for raccoon's sake.

8. Wash hands after handling for your own sake.

HOT TIPS FOR RACCOONS

1. In the case of found babies, watch for mother first: DON'T RACCOONNAP while mother is looking for food.

2. Warm raccoon first in your hands, or against your body.

3. Put in warm, quiet place.

4. Generally, it's a good idea to give rehydration solution before food.

5. NEVER FEED a cold, starving raccoon or any other critter before warming and rehydrating.

6. Keep household pets away however gentle. Raccoons and other small wildlife need to learn to fear cats and dogs.

7. Call Department of Environmental Protection, or your local wildlife rehabilitator, for advice and help. Your vet or local police will have telephone numbers.

Reference books:

PETERSON FIELD GUIDE SERIES, A Field Guide to the Mammals of North America north of Mexico, A Field Guide to Birds (regional), by Roger Tory Peterson, Houghton, Mifflin Company, Boston.

STOKES NATURE GUIDES, A Guide to Animal Tracking and Behavior, A Guide to Bird Behavior, Volume I,II,III, by Donald Stokes, Little, Brown and Company, Boston.

AUDUBON HANDBOOKS, Mcgraw-Hill Book Company, New York, San Francisco, Singapore, Toronto, et al.

Recommended manuals:

WILDLIFE RESCUE, INC., Austin, Texas.

WILDLIFE CARE AND REHABILITATION, Brukner Nature Center, Troy, Ohio.

WILD ANIMAL CARE AND REHABILITATION, The Kalamazoo Nature Center, Kalamazoo, Michigan.

BASIC WILDLIFE REHABILITATION, 1AB, International Wildlife Rehabilitation Council, Suisun, California.

INTRODUCTION TO WILDLIFE REHABILITATION, National Wildlife Rehabilitators Association, Carpenter Nature Center, Hastings, Minnesota.

Notes

Notes

BICK
PUBLISHING HOUSE
PRESENTS
WIND OVER WINGS PRESS

BASIC MANUAL
WILDLIFE REHABILITATION SERIES
IN 6 VOLUMES

ISBN: 1-884158-00-5
Volume 1
Price: $6.25

ISBN: 1-884158-03-x
Volume 4
Price $6.25

ISBN: 1-884158-01-3
Volume 2
Price $6.25

ISBN: 1-884158-06-4
Volume 5
Price $6.25

ISBN: 884158-02-1
Volume 3
Price $6.25

ISBN: 1-884158-05-6
Volume 6
Price $6.25

- For parents, teachers, librarians who want to learn and teach basic rehabilitation
- For backyard rehabilitators
- For rehabilitation centers, to sell to volunteers

Order from your local bookstore through:
BAKER & TAYLOR
INLAND BOOK COMPANY
or by writing or calling:
WILDLIFE REHABILITATION TODAY MAGAZINE
Coconut Creek Publishing Co.
2201 NW 40TH Terrace
Coconut Creek, FL 33066
(305) 972-6092

- Perfect bound editions available ■